SALTSHAKE

Spirituality According to Jesus

*8 Seeker Bible Discussions
on the Gospel of Luke*

Rebecca Manley Pippert

InterVarsity Press
Downers Grove, Illinois
Leicester, England

InterVarsity Press, USA
P.O. Box 1400, Downers Grove, IL 60515-1426, USA
World Wide Web: www.ivpress.com
E-mail: mail@ivpress.com

Inter-Varsity Press, England
38 De Montfort Street, Leicester LE1 7GP, England
World Wide Web: www.ivpbooks.com
E-mail: ivp@uccf.org.uk

InterVarsity Press®, U.S.A., is the book-publishing division of InterVarsity Christian
Fellowship/USA®, a student movement active on campus at hundreds of
universities, colleges and schools of nursing in the United States of America, and a
member movement of the International Fellowship of Evangelical Students. For
information about local and regional activities, write Public Relations Dept.,
InterVarsity Christian Fellowship/USA, 6400 Schroeder Rd., P.O. Box 7895,
Madison, WI 53707-7895, or visit the IVCF website at <www.intervarsity.org>.

Inter-Varsity Press, England, is the book-publishing division of the Universities and
Colleges Christian Fellowship (formerly the Inter-Varsity Fellowship), a student
movement linking Christian Unions in universities and colleges throughout the
United Kingdom and the Republic of Ireland, and a member movement of the
International Fellowship of Evangelical Students. For information about local and
national activities write to UCCF, 38 De Montfort Street, Leicester LE1 7GP.

Design: Cindy Kiple

Images: Macduff Everton/Getty Images

USA ISBN 0-8308-2125-2

UK ISBN 1-84474-058-7

Printed in the United States of America ∞

P	16	15	14	13	12	11	10	9	8	7	6	5	4	3	2	1
Y	16	15	14	13	12	11	10	09	08	07	06	05	04			

CONTENTS

INTRODUCTION

It is astonishing to reflect on the rise of spirituality in recent years. Twenty years ago we didn't even have names for spiritual practices that are considered commonplace today. Indeed, it is unusual to find people who *don't* consider themselves "spiritual" people.

What our spiritual age has revealed is our awareness of an inner emptiness. We now know that we can have an abundance of sex, food and wealth, and still be miserable. Certainly the plethora of self-help Anonymous meetings that have sprung up in recent years around every conceivable vice is further evidence that we are looking for something we haven't yet found.

It's clear we are searching for something worth living for, and for some way to be at peace with ourselves, to calm our inner conflicts, and solve our dissatisfaction with life and with ourselves. We want to be happy and we want to be loved. But what we cannot understand is why something so simple should be so difficult. As Mark Twain once reflected, "You don't know quite what it is you do want, but it just fairly makes your heart ache you want it so."

But how are we to fill our inner spiritual emptiness? That is where the confusion lies, especially when there are so many options before us. We may try crystal therapy, finding our "inner child," doing Quantum healing, celebrating the earth goddess or swimming with dolphins. Yet the feeling remains that somehow we were made for something more. There is more for us to live for, to embrace and to be embraced by.

I am sure that no one writes a book who does not have some truth to share. I am no exception. For many years I was a seeker who longed to feel "connected" to the cosmic whole. I questioned if it were possible to restore not only my own sense of brokenness but was there hope, I wondered, for this battered earth with all its wounded people?

The truth that has changed my life was coming to believe in God as shown in Jesus Christ. But I did not start from faith. On the contrary, I made my pilgrimage from unbelief to faith, kicking and resisting all the way. And since my own journey began in skepticism, where I was encouraged to ask questions and never asked to adopt belief blindly, I have chosen a similar approach in these Bible discussions. It is not necessary that you believe in Jesus or accept the Bible as "divinely inspired" in order to use this guide. Rather, come to the accounts of Jesus as you would to any sound history, with an open mind and heart to see what you find.

Using This Discussion Guide

This guide is written to encourage give-and-take group discussion led by a moderator. The open-style discussion challenges you as participants to wrestle with the text yourselves and to reach your own conclusions. Don't feel intimidated if this is your first time reading the Bible; that means your contributions to group discussions will be fresh and stimulating. Remember, there is no homework. If you want to answer the questions ahead of time go right ahead (space is provided for writing answers to each question). If you are able to read the passage ahead of time, then do so. But it's also fine to simply show up each week without having prepared ahead of time.

Each session has several components. The "Discussion Starter" question is simply meant to kick off the discussion for a few minutes. The "Historical Context" section is intended to be read aloud. Its purpose is to provide background to the Scripture. Other historical information is found here and there amidst the discussion questions. The "Discovering Jesus" section contains questions that help us engage the text in order to understand its meaning. The "Live What You Learn" section is to help us apply the truth we've studied to our everyday lives.

This guide is based on the Gospel of Luke. Why study the Gospel of Luke? Because Luke's Gospel is tailor-made for our pluralistic culture. Luke was most likely not a Jew but a Gentile. Therefore he was particularly interested in the spread of the good news beyond the bounds of the Israelite nation. Most of us in the Western world are the kinds of people Luke was addressing in the first century. Early church tradition has consistently named Luke as the author of both the Gospel and the book of Acts. Although there is some debate as to the precise date this Gospel was written, many scholars believe it was written during the early 60s of the first century.

Luke was a physician by trade and perhaps because of that he was concerned with how Jesus' message affected human needs—spiritually, emotionally and physically. But beyond the great humanity of the text, Luke was equally clear about the supernatural dimension of Jesus. That is why his Gospel begins with all manner of supernatural occurrences. Luke wants us to understand that we can not understand the gospel message of Jesus Christ without understanding its spiritual origins. Why did Luke begin his Gospel as he did? Because he wanted to show that God had broken into our world for the first time. The good news didn't have its origins in earth but in heaven!

ONE

LUKE 1:1-38

Preparing for Jesus

◆ Discussion Starter

Just suppose that God truly exists and desires to communicate with us. If you were God and decided to perform a supernatural break-in on planet earth, how would you go about it?

◆ Historical Context

Christianity is a religion of revelation. It begins with the assumption that God exists and has broken into our world through the coming of Christ. That is why the announcement of his birth is first proclaimed from heaven—not earth. If there is no God, then these angelic proclamations are preposterous. But if there *is* a God, then why wouldn't God confirm this supernatural break-in through extraordinary means?

All through the Old Testament we see God's promises to send a Messiah who would pay for the sins of the world. Furthermore, these Old Testament prophecies say that, before the Messiah appears, a forerunner would come to prepare the way (Isaiah 40:3-8). But much time has passed since these prophecies were told. The Jewish people have been under the domination of foreign empires since 587 B.C.: first the Babylonians, Medo-Persians, Greeks and now the Romans. There had been no prophet for 400 years—until John the Baptist!

We are about to read a passage in which we see faithful people face extraordinary events. Zechariah and Elizabeth, Mary and Joseph are godly people whose faith is about to be tested severely: Will they trust God's Word or their present circumstances?

◆ Discovering Jesus

An Angel Visits: Read Luke 1:1-25.

1. What was Luke's method in writing, and what was his purpose (vv. 3-4)?

2. What does Luke tell us about Zechariah and Elizabeth (vv. 5-7)?

As one of about 18,000 priests, Zechariah would serve in the temple twice a year, but only once in his life would he get to assist in the daily offering by going into the Holy Place. Most of the priests would never have this privilege, and no one was allowed to do it twice. It was determined by lot, and this time the lot fell on Zechariah! His job was to go into the temple alone and offer incense on the golden altar in the Holy Place. While the priest was inside, huge crowds waited outside and the people would watch, and when they saw the smoke of the incense rising up out of the altar, they were to prostrate themselves in prayer. The priest would say a set prayer as he offered the incense. After Zechariah had offered the incense he was required to go out to the waiting people and pronounce a blessing on the crowd.

3. How was Gabriel's message of good news an answer to two prayers that Zechariah must have prayed over the years (v. 13)?

4. What did the angel say about the child that Zechariah and Elizabeth would have (vv. 13-17)?

5. What is Zechariah's response to this news in verse 18? What miracle convinced Zechariah that what Gabriel said was true (vv. 20-22)?

6. How might the discipline of silence be a gift to Zechariah during this season of his life?

7. What was Elizabeth's response to her pregnancy (vv. 23-25)?

The Birth of Jesus Foretold: Read Luke 1:26-38.

8. In the sixth month of Elizabeth's pregnancy, Gabriel appeared to Mary (vv. 26-31). What do you think must have gone through Mary's mind when Gabriel appeared to her? (Note what Gabriel says to her in verse 28.)

9. What did Gabriel tell Mary about Jesus and his birth (vv. 31-33)?

10. What does the text tell us about Mary?

11. What does Gabriel say that calms Mary's fears and questions (vv. 35-37)?

12. How would you compare and contrast Mary's response to Zechariah's response (v. 38)?

Prophecy Fulfilled: Read Luke 1:57-66.

13. Describe how Zechariah's voice was restored (vv. 62-64).

14. Note that the name John means "God be praised" or "gift from God." What was the result of Zechariah's action (vv. 65-66)?

15. Luke is an objective historian writing to Theophilus, who is either a Gentile seeker or a very new convert to Christianity. You would think Luke would want to avoid bringing up such controversial topics as angels, prophets and miracles to a Gentile who would be suspicious of the supernatural. Why do you think God used an angel to announce both John's and Jesus' births?

◆ Live What You Learn

16. We often assume that it was easier to believe in biblical times. Yet in this passage we see Zechariah, a godly man, wrestle with doubt and skepticism. Even Mary, who is a model believer, did not comprehend fully all that was happening to her at this stage. What is it about Zechariah and Mary's journey of faith that gives you hope as you wrestle with your own questions about God?

TWO

Presenting Jesus

◆ Discussion Starter

If the United States were to transition from a democracy to a monarchy and the one who would be the first king or queen were about to be born, what would you expect the parents to be like? In what circumstances would you expect the baby to be born?

◆ Historical Context

Matthew 1:18-25 gives us more details about Joseph. It is clear Joseph assumed Mary had been unfaithful. Because he was a good man, he wanted to protect Mary from disgrace and decided to divorce her quietly. (An engagement was a legal agreement.) What changed his mind? An angel appeared to him in a dream and told him what to name the child and that the child conceived in Mary was from the Holy Spirit. Perhaps he recalled the Old Testament prophecies that the Messiah would be born of a virgin. One of the names of this child was to be *Immanuel* ("God with us") which is literally true beyond anything they could imagine.

After the angel Gabriel told Mary and Joseph the news that they would have a son who would be Messiah, they eventually traveled south from Nazareth to register with the Roman census in Bethlehem. Caesar Augustus (Octavian), who ruled from 27 B.C. to A.D. 14, ordered a census requiring all Romans and Jews to register in their hometowns. The census was a procedure to get a registration list for taxes—a painful reminder to Jews of their Roman occupation.

The trip from Nazareth to Bethlehem was ninety miles, at least a three-day journey by foot. The timing couldn't have seemed more inconvenient for this young couple with a baby on the way. But God had a deeper plan in mind that he was fulfilling; for in Micah 5:1-2 it was prophesied some 700 years before Christ's birth that their promised ruler and deliverer would come out of Bethlehem.

The fact that Luke dates the birth of Jesus by carefully telling us who the Roman ruler and governor were indicates that he is writing about true history, not myth. Luke wants us to know that this isn't an allegory to teach us a truth—this is historical fact.

◆ Discovering Jesus

The Birth of Jesus: Read Luke 2:1-7.

1.   Describe the circumstances of Jesus' birth.

2. If Jesus really is God's Son sent from heaven, then what do you think is the significance of such a humble birth (see Philippians 2:5-11)?

The Shepherds and the Angels: Read Luke 2:8-20.

3. Describe what the shepherds saw and how they re-acted (vv. 8-12).

4. Why do you think the birth announcement was made to shepherds?

5. What is the significance of the names given to Jesus in verse 11?

6. What character traits do you notice in Joseph and Mary (vv. 4, 5, 16-19)?

Jesus Presented in the Temple: Read Luke 2:21-40.

7. When Mary and Joseph enter the temple to dedicate Jesus, they meet Simeon and Anna (vv. 25-38). What were they like?

8. What had the Holy Spirit revealed to Simeon about Jesus' life purpose (vv. 29-32)?

9. What additional prophecy did Simeon give to Mary about her son (vv. 34-35)?

10. How must Mary and Joseph have felt as they heard what Simeon had to say as he held their baby?

11. From verse 40 how would you picture Jesus as a child?

The Boy Jesus at the Temple: Read Luke 2:41-52.

12. What do you learn about Jesus in his meeting with the nation's top biblical scholars (vv. 46-47)?

13. What more do you learn about Jesus' sense of identity and mission from his response to Mary's gentle rebuke (vv. 48-50)?

14. Luke probably interviewed Mary about the early years of Jesus. If so, what do you think she said about these years (vv. 51-52)?

◆ Live What You Learn

15. Mary had to face enormous challenges in her life. She would lose her husband and her son while she was still young. Yet she demonstrated a trust and serenity that is remarkable. What stands out to you about Mary that you want to emulate?

THREE

LUKE 3:21-23; 4:1-30

The Power of
Good over Evil

◆ Discussion Starter

Temptation is a fascinating subject that rarely gets the
attention it should, especially considering it's such a
universal problem. "I can resist anything but temptation," the saying goes. To be clear, temptation must not
be confused with sin. Even Jesus was tempted, as we
will see in this passage, but he did not sin. Rather,
temptation is what occurs when we still have a choice
to make between choosing the good over the wrong.

Why do you think people are so vulnerable to temptation?

Have you found any strategies that help you deal
with temptation?

◆ Historical Context

Thirty years have passed since John was born to very
elderly parents. Luke moves his account forward in

time about seventeen years to the beginning of John the Baptist's ministry. For the previous year or so, John the Baptist has been preaching in the country around the Jordan River about a baptism of repentance for the forgiveness of sins. He preached that the Messiah was coming soon, and that anyone (Jew or Gentile) could be prepared for his coming if they acknowledged their sin and turned to godly living. Some Jewish aristocrats disagreed with John saying that only Gentiles would be judged and punished when the Messiah came. But John insisted that *all* needed repentance.

Some thought John was the Messiah, but he refuted these claims, explaining that his purpose was to prepare the way for Messiah. John had been shown by God that the identifying sign of the Christ would be the Spirit descending in a form like a dove upon him (John 1:32-34). But then one day Jesus turned up in the crowd to be baptized, and John experienced the high point of his life—the purpose for which he was born.

◆ Discovering Jesus

Jesus' Baptism: Read Luke 3:21-23.

1. Picture the scene at Jesus' baptism. What did Jesus see and hear at his baptism (3:21-22)?

2. What significance would it have on Jesus to hear this divine endorsement from both God the Father

and God the Holy Spirit who participated in Jesus' ordination?

3. John's baptism was intended to demonstrate the need for repentance and moral reform in preparation for the Messiah who would baptize with the Holy Spirit. If Jesus is God's Son and therefore sinless, then why did he choose to be baptized?

God guided Jesus into the desert for forty days because he was testing his character and strengthening him through trials to be ready for his unique ministry. Forty is a significant number in the Bible. Israel wandered for forty years; the flood lasted for forty days; Moses and Elijah fasted for forty days at key points in their ministries. Often when that number appears significant events occur.

Jesus Tempted in the Desert: Read Luke 4:1-13.

4. In verse 3 Satan challenges Jesus' true identity by saying, "If you are the Son of God . . ." Why do you think the first temptation had to do with food (4:1-4)?

5. Why would it have been wrong for Jesus to do what the devil asked?

6. How did Jesus respond to the devil's second temptation (4:5-8)?

7. What new tactic did the devil try in the third temptation (4:9-11)?

8. What do you think gave Jesus the power to withstand Satan?

Jesus Rejected at Nazareth: Read Luke 4:14-30.

9. What do you think it would have been like for Jesus to return to his hometown?

10. Describe Jesus' physical movements as he prepared to read. What would it have felt like to be present in that moment?

11. What do we learn about Jesus' identity and mission from his teaching (4:18-21)?

   When Jesus made his claim (4:21) what was the response of the audience (4:22)?

12. What did Jesus say to enrage the people in the synagogue (4:24-27)?

13. Why do you think Jesus was able to walk right through the crowd and escape lynching (4:30)?

◆ Live What You Learn

14. All of us struggle with temptation, and Jesus was no exception. Bookstores are crammed with popular self-help books. What new strategies have you learned from Jesus about dealing with temptation?

FOUR

LUKE 4:31–5:11

The Power of Jesus Released

◇ Discussion Starter

We all wear many hats and we have many demands placed on us from all sides. How do you keep a sense of what's most important and remain centered amidst the pressures of life?

◆ Historical Context

Jesus was still in the early months of his ministry. His preparation had been completed through his study of the Jewish law since he was twelve, his baptism at thirty, and his subsequent fasting and resistance to the temptations in the desert. His identity was confirmed by divine announcement at his baptism. Then Jesus claimed to be the fulfillment of the messianic prophecy in Isaiah during a hometown visit at his Nazareth synagogue. His townspeople responded in disbelief and rejected him. Jesus now made Capernaum his base of operations. The text logs a twenty-four-hour day in the life of Jesus as he revealed his power and authority over evil, sickness and nature. Take note of the varied human needs that Jesus answers.

◆ Discovering Jesus

Jesus the Healer: Read Luke 4:31-44.

1. What is the people's response to Jesus' teaching (v. 32)?

2. Describe what took place in 4:33-34 from the perspective of an onlooker.

3. Who do you think was addressing Jesus—the man or the evil spirit inside of him (vv. 33-34)?

   What did the demon know about Jesus?

4. After commanding the evil spirit to come out, why do you think Jesus silenced the demon when it had spoken the truth and attested to the true identity of Jesus?

5. We have just seen Jesus' authority over evil powers. Now we see his power over physical illness (vv. 38-39). Why was Jesus able to do this?

6. What strikes you as significant about Jesus' ministry to the townspeople (vv. 40-41)?

7. In the midst of a very busy ministry that day, what were Jesus' clear priorities the following morning (vv. 42-44)?

8. What reasons did Jesus give for his need to move on (v. 43)?

Calling of the First Disciples: Read Luke 5:1-11.

The fishermen in this passage had been following Jesus and traveling with him for a while. The other Gospels reveal that by now they had seen several miracles and a great many healings. No doubt each time they returned to Capernaum, Peter, Andrew, James and John—who were business partners along with John's father, Zebedee—returned to their fishing. This was probably not a small business since there were also hired employees.

9. Describe what is going on in 5:1-3. (What is Jesus doing? What are the disciples doing? What is the crowd like?)

10. Jesus got into Simon's boat (v. 3), and since Peter didn't take the hint, Jesus made his request. How might Simon have felt about this interruption?

11. If Jesus' first request was inconvenient, consider how Jesus' second request might have sounded to Peter. List various reasons Peter would have preferred not to comply.

12. What indications are there that this was an incredibly large catch of fish (5:4-9)?

13. How would you explain the effect this miracle had on Peter?

14. What third request did Jesus make, and what did it mean (see also Mark 1:16-20)?

15. What have these men seen about Jesus that would give them the confidence to quit their business and follow him unreservedly?

◆ Live What You Learn

16. Jesus had a remarkable sense of purpose and priorities. It enabled him to know what to say no to, and it provided him with calmness and courage as he faced enormous challenges. What do you think you might have to say no to or leave behind in order to follow Christ?

FIVE

LUKE 5:12-31

The Power of Jesus Revealed

◈ Discussion Starter

What are common stereotypes that people have about Christians?

◆ Historical Context

So far in Luke we have studied Jesus' *preparation* for ministry and the revelation of his *power* over evil, sickness and nature. Now Jesus begins to reveal the *purpose* of his coming as he clashes with the religious authorities in Palestine.

There are several types of religious leaders in Jesus' day. We'll meet two of them in this reading. The Pharisees, whose name means "separated ones," were a separatist and legalistic group who strictly kept the Law of Moses (the first five books of the Bible). They were teachers in the synagogues, religious examples for the people, and self-appointed guardians of the law and its observance. The second group, the teachers of the law, were not all Pharisees but were professionally trained in teaching and applying the law. Both groups believed that God's grace only extended to those who kept the law, which involved knowledge, vigilance and sacrifice. Jesus' actions in these five encounters challenged their assumptions, as Jesus began to teach more directly about sin.

In the first set of verses we meet a leper. In Jesus' day to have leprosy made one a total outcast from society. However leprosy wasn't an exact diagnosis. It was also used to describe those with inflammatory or scaly skin diseases. This man must have had ugly skin ulcerations all over his body.

◆ Discovering Jesus

Jesus Heals a Leper: Read Luke 5:12-16.

1. It was forbidden for a leper to walk right into the presence of a non-leper. What do you think gave him the courage to take this risk?

2. How did Jesus respond to the leper (v. 13; see also Mark 1:41)?

3. What is significant about how Jesus healed the leper?

4. Jesus instructed the man not to tell anyone of the incident but to immediately carry out the Jewish ritual for cleansing so that he could be reinstated into the community (v. 14). Why did Jesus tell him not to tell anyone?

5. What effect would this healing have had on the man's relationships to his family and community?

What effect did this healing have on Jesus' ministry?

Jesus Heals the Paralytic: Read Luke 5:17-26.

6. Look closely at who is present in verse 17 and where they come from. Why do you think the Pharisees and teachers of the law decided to come at the same time?

7. Describe the scene as the paralyzed man is lowered into the room. What was it about the paralytic's friends that impressed Jesus (v. 20)?

8. Jesus makes a surprising statement—"Your sins are forgiven" (v. 20)—before healing the paralytic. Why would this be welcome news to this suffering man?

9. Why did the religious dignitaries believe Jesus had committed blasphemy (v. 21)?

10. What justification did Jesus make for his claim?

11. Describe the scene in verses 24-26 when the paralytic responds to Jesus' impossible command.

Jesus Calls Levi: Read Luke 5:27-31.

Tax collectors were Jewish agents for the Roman government. Jews detested them for helping a pagan conqueror and for frequently defrauding their own people. Levi's tax booth was probably like a tollbooth, set up on an international road from Damascus through Capernaum to the Mediterranean coast and Egypt. After he became Jesus' disciple, Levi's name was changed to Matthew, and he later wrote one of the four Gospels.

12. Why would Jesus ask a hated outcast to be one of his disciples (vv. 27-31)?

13. It seems clear from Levi's response that he must have heard and observed Jesus for some time. In view of his unsavory life, why did Levi then leave everything without hesitation to follow Jesus?

14. Why, as a new believer, did Levi throw a huge party and invite such a disreputable lot for Jesus to meet?

15. Why did the Pharisees and teachers of the law show up at Levi's party?

What was Jesus' answer to their criticism?

◆ Live What You Learn

16. In this passage we see that Jesus offered help for the whole person: he healed the leper and freed him to no longer be an outcast; he forgave the sins of the paralytic; and he offered salvation to all, even the despised tax collector. As you look at the chart that follows, reflect on the preconceived notions that Jesus challenged in his day. Then ask: Have any of my preconceived notions about what it means to follow Christ been challenged? Talk about why or why not.

Verses	Jesus' Radical Action	Assumptions He Challenged	A New Way of Thinking About God
5:17-26	He claimed authority to forgive sin.	Jesus is not God. God cannot become man.	God became man to reveal who he is to us, and he wants to forgive our sins.
5:27-28	He called an outcast to follow him.	Only pious people join a religious leader. Tax collectors cannot expect salvation.	God does not wait for us to do something good to earn his favor. He wants us as we are now.
5:29-32	He socialized with crooks and immoral community rejects.	These people are beyond redemption.	Nobody is beyond having a close, personal relationship with God.

SIX

The Plan for True Living

◇ Discussion Starter

The Catholic writer G. K. Chesterton once remarked, considering Christ's commands to love our enemies and pray for those who persecute us: "Christianity isn't just difficult—it's *impossible*." Do you agree or disagree and why?

◆ Historical Context

Up until now Jesus had been universally popular with common people and religious leaders alike. But once Jesus forgave the sins of the paralytic in Luke 5, the religious leaders became increasingly critical. In chapter 6 the tension between them is at fever pitch and would remain so for the rest of Jesus' ministry. The religious leaders were upset that Jesus and his disciples were not honoring the sabbath by eating grain as they passed through a field. They were troubled when Jesus healed a man with a shriveled arm because they felt these acts constituted "work," which was unlawful to do on the sabbath. Jesus not only defeated their arguments but he claimed to be the Lord of the Sabbath himself (that is, to have authority over it). He not only claimed to be Messiah but also claimed he represented the new Israel, the people of a new covenant, which the prophets had predicted. He was replacing the Jewish sabbath rules with a new kind of sabbath, and replacing the old law with a new one.

As the tension mounted Jesus chose twelve apostles whom he would work and travel with closely. These people would be the leaders of a new community of faith and would carry on his work after he was gone. How should this new community of believers live? Beginning in Luke 6:20 Jesus addresses his disciples with some important information about the way that they are to conduct themselves.

◆ Discovering Jesus

Love for Enemies: Read Luke 6:27-36.

1. List the ways Jesus described our enemies. What radical standards did Jesus call his disciples to follow (vv. 27-31)? Describe what they were to do in every case.

2. Verse 31 says, "Do to others as you would have them do to you." Give a positive or negative example in regard to how you have succeeded or failed in this task.

3. Look at verses 32-34. What outcome do you think it would have on our relationships if we practiced Jesus' guidelines for behavior? Think about this from both our perspective and our enemies' perspective.

4. What reasons did Jesus give for loving our enemies (vv. 35-36)?

5. How would this teaching be particularly relevant to the disciples?

Judging Others: Read Luke 6:37-45.

6. In what circumstances did Jesus teach that it made good sense to exercise judgment (vv. 39-40, 42, 45)?

7. From your experience do you agree or disagree with what Jesus was saying here and why?

8. At the same time Jesus says, "Do not judge" (v. 37). What do you think Jesus was getting at?

9. All through this passage Jesus is talking to the newly chosen disciples. Consider their circumstances. Why might they be tempted to criticize each other?

10. Why was it so important to Jesus that his disciples should have loving relationships?

11. What did Jesus say should temper our tendency to quickly judge one another (v. 41)?

12. That Jesus was not absolutely forbidding all judging can be seen in the story about the tree and its fruit. Why is good fruit a helpful way to gauge a person's character?

13. Jesus acknowledged the lack of character in his enemies and encouraged us to do so (vv. 43-45). Why, in your opinion, is it important for us to be able to acknowledge evil when we see or experience it?

14. What benefits come from not taking it on ourselves to judge, condemn or withhold forgiveness from those we are in conflict with (vv. 37-38)?

◆ Live What You Learn

15. Think of a person who you have been in conflict with. What principles do you think Jesus would follow if he were in your shoes?

16. Verse 28 says, "Pray for those who mistreat you." How would it be helpful to pray for the person you are in conflict with?

SEVEN

The Power to Overcome Suffering

◆ Discussion Starter

If you were told you had six months to live, how would you prepare your loved ones to face life with courage and to live life well without you?

◆ Historical Context

In the first cluster of miracles we read about in Luke chapters 4 and 5, we saw Jesus' power over evil, whether in mind, body or circumstance. We also saw that there were nearly always large crowds around.

Now we are about to read of another cluster of miracles and again we will see the power Jesus has over evil. Only this time there are no crowds watching the miracles, nor are the onlookers merely casual observers. This time the miracles are performed for the benefit of his disciples alone, his committed followers. Why the change? In chapter 6 Jesus appointed twelve new leaders to represent a new community of faith. Jesus knows that his days are numbered and he is preparing his disciples to follow in his footsteps after he is gone.

Jesus has been ministering in Capernaum, and Mark's Gospel (4:35) informs us that when evening came Jesus left the crowds and told his disciples that he wanted to cross the lake. But this was not a trip simply to Bethsaida, but to the region of the Gerasenes where the Gentiles lived. This was one of ten towns that made up the Decapolis, which was directly under Roman jurisdiction. To get to this region they would have to cross the lake from its northwest corner to its southeast corner (more than thirteen miles).

◆ Discovering Jesus

The Storm on the Lake: Read Luke 8:22-25.

1. Considering these were experienced fishermen very accustomed to fierce storms on this lake, their panic suggests that this was a particularly fierce storm. How could Jesus have slept through such a terrible storm?

2. When Jesus woke up, he mildly rebuked the disciples for lacking faith. What had he told them when they set out that they now doubted (v. 22)?

3. After Jesus performed this miracle, why were the disciples afraid (v. 25)?

The Healing of a Demon-Possessed Man: Read Luke 8:26-39.

4. How would you describe the state of the Gerasene man (vv. 27-29)?

5. Why do you think Jesus asked him his name?

The Abyss is found in Revelation 9:1 and is a place reserved for the devil and all his demons. The demons feared extinction, which is why they wanted to seek something to inhabit.

6. What did the townspeople see when they returned to where Jesus was (vv. 35, 38-39)?

7. How does the fear expressed by the Gerasenes in verse 37 differ from the disciples' fear in verse 25?

Jesus doesn't impose his presence where it is not desired, so he leaves. However, Jesus still extends grace to the community by leaving behind a man whose life had been totally transformed by him.

Jairus's Daughter and a Sick Woman: Read Luke 8:40-56. Jesus and his disciples are back in home territory in Capernaum. Jesus has not even gotten out of the boat (Mark 5:21) when a large crowd gathers to welcome him.

8. Why might the crowd be surprised that Jairus would fall at Jesus' feet with a desperate plea for help?

9. Jesus seems to have left for Jairus's home immediately. Describe the condition of the woman who interrupts Jesus on the way (v. 43).

10. How was Jesus able to distinguish an inadvertent touch from a touch of faith (v. 46)?

11. The woman had come up behind Jesus, hoping she wouldn't be noticed. Why was she trembling in fear when she realized she had been discovered (v. 47)?

12. How does Jesus respond to this young woman who reached out in faith (vv. 37, 48)?

13. Meanwhile how do you suppose Jairus is feeling during these events and upon hearing the news in verse 49?

14. What astounding words of hope does Jesus give Jairus (v. 50)?

15. Why does Jesus only allow the three disciples and the parents into the young girl's room when he performs the miracle?

   Why does Jesus command the parents not to tell how this happened?

Jesus is training and preparing his disciples to live wisely and well after he is gone. He wants his disciples to understand that following him isn't receiving an exemption card from life's difficulties. Evil is a reality in this life and Christians must know how to confront it. That is why Jesus forces them to confront a horrifying storm, the diseased mind of a demoniac, a devastating illness and a corpse. All were situations beyond human hope. Jesus seems to be saying, "Though you enjoy being my followers, you still live in a world where evil exists. How will you face it?"

◆ Live What You Learn

16. Jesus makes it clear that we will neither be free *from* trials in this life, nor do we have to be helpless *in* trials. How are we to find the power to cope *with* life's difficulties according to Jesus?

EIGHT

LUKE 9:10-36

Who Do You Say That I Am?

◆ **Discussion Starter**

Who has most influenced your life and what did they do that was so effective?

◆ **Historical Context**

Luke 9 marks a new phase of Jesus' ministry. Jesus had selected twelve men from among his followers to be his apostles, special representatives to the world who would become the leaders of the early church. To prepare them for their task, Jesus spent most of his time from this point on, training and teaching them. This chapter begins with Jesus sending out his twelve disciples in twos (Mark 6:7) to saturate Galilee, doing the type of preaching, teaching and healing that they had observed Jesus doing. Jesus gave them his own power and authority to minister. He instructs them to go with no extra resources, trusting God to provide their needs through people in the various towns. Their outreach was an enormous success. Jesus and his message were noticed everywhere. In Luke 9:7 we see that even King Herod Antipas, (the son of Herod the Great), the Roman ruler over Galilee and Perea who resided in Jerusalem, wondered who this Jesus of Nazareth was. Herod had already executed John the Baptist so his interest in Jesus' ministry signals an increased danger to Jesus' mission. Upon their return Jesus led the apostles to a secluded area for a retreat.

◆ Discovering Jesus

Jesus Feeds the Five Thousand: Read Luke 9:10-17.

1. How would you describe Jesus' attitude toward the crowd (vv. 10-11)?

    What do you think the disciples were feeling as they saw the crowd? (See Mark 6:31-34.)

2. The disciples have just completed a very successful missionary journey in which they had witnessed many miracles and God's provision. Yet what tests of faith did they fail here (vv. 12-14)?

3. What progressive steps does Jesus take in involving the disciples in this miracle (vv. 12-17)?

4. What do you think the crowd was feeling when Jesus gave thanks for the food (v. 16)?

5. What did Jesus teach the disciples through this miracle (which included picking up the surplus, v. 17)?

Peter's Confession of Christ: Read Luke 9:18-27.

6. What two questions does Jesus ask the disciples (vv. 18, 20)?

7. What is significant about how Simon Peter answers the question (v. 20; see also Matthew 16:16)?

8. Why does Jesus command them not to tell anyone (9:21; see John 6:15)?

9. His disciples must have hoped that Jesus would now use his supernatural powers to free the Jewish people from Roman domination. How would they have felt about Jesus' next revelation about himself (v. 22)?

10. In verse 23 Jesus tells them what it means to be his faithful follower. Why does he tell his disciples to do this (vv. 24-25)?

11. What does Jesus say are the benefits to these short-time costs (vv. 26-27)?

The Transfiguration: Read Luke 9:28-36.

12. How does this incident fulfill the prophecy in Luke 9:27?

13. What did Peter, James and John see when Jesus took them on the mountain to pray (vv. 28-31)?

14. Moses and Elijah spoke to Jesus of his death from an eternal perspective. Moses had been the great Old Testament recorder and witness of the law, and Elijah was the greatest of the prophets of the Old Testament. Both men affirmed that Jesus was the fulfillment of their ministries (for example, the Law and the Prophets of the Old Testament). When Moses and Elijah begin to depart how does Peter try to detain them (v. 33)?

15. What would be the significance of this event for Jesus and for the disciples (v. 35)?

For once even Peter could not speak the experience was so overwhelming and awe producing. It would be years later before Peter would write about this event (2 Peter 1:16-18).

◆ Live What You Learn

16. If Jesus asked you, "Who do you say that I am?" how would you respond at this point in your spiritual journey?

LEADER'S NOTES

Here's a little background on how the studies are put together and how to use each component.

Discussion Starter: Use this as an icebreaker to help people feel comfortable. The question addresses everyday concerns as well as an issue that relates to the biblical text. Why do we ask a general question first? Seekers often feel intimidated about reading the Bible. They are afraid their lack of Bible knowledge will show, or they feel hesitant to ask or give an honest response. But if *you* are relaxed and begin the study each week with a provocative question, it will lighten the atmosphere and make the participants feel at ease. Don't spend more than three minutes on the opening question. After discussing the question, there are several sentences you may read that will lead you into the "Historical Context" section.

Historical Context: This gives the participants some historical or cultural background in order to better understand the passage. Sometimes it merely explains what has happened in previous chapters. You may summarize the information or read it aloud while they read along with you (the participants should each have a guide). Remember, our role as leaders is not to be a "sage on the stage—but a guide on the side."

Discovering Jesus: These are questions that follow the inductive method. This is an approach that helps them discover, understand and correlate the facts in the text and discover for themselves what the Scripture is saying. One distinctive of a seeker Bible discussion is that the questions do not assume faith on the part of the participant. However, the questions engage the reader to look carefully at the text in order to understand its meaning.

Live What You Learn: These are the application questions. You will notice that as each week progresses the questions become a bit more focused and direct. Try to get through the passage so there's enough time to ask the application question. The more you get everyone participating in the conversation the better. Remember, however, to set the time for your study and stick to it. I would recommend no longer than sixty minutes.

Reading the Passage

You may wonder whether to read the entire passage first or read by sections and ask questions that pertain to each section. That depends on how long the passage is. In these studies I have broken each passage into sections so that you can read the Scripture in small units for better comprehension. Also, ask if anyone would like to read but don't call on someone to read. If no one offers to read then ask your coleader or read it yourself.

What to Do at Your First Study

There are two ways to start a study. One way is to have an introductory meeting. Keep it fun and offer light refreshments and introduce everyone to each other. Then explain your purpose in gathering and select a time to gather that works for everyone. Then hand out the studies and ask them to read the passage ahead of time if they wish. But assure them that "homework" isn't required. If they want to answer the questions in the guide they may; reading the text ahead of time will be helpful. But if they don't have time to do either, that's okay. You don't want them to stay away if they haven't read the passage, especially since you'll be reading it when you meet. Also discover if everyone has a Bible and if they don't you can suggest a particular translation. I suggest RSV and NIV.

The other approach is to figure out through conversations which time seems to work for everyone and invite them to come. At the first meeting be sure you have extra Bibles. No one will have read the passage but that's okay. Before you study the passage be sure to review the purpose for gathering and go over a few of the ground rules. Then after the study you may hand out the Bible study guide and tell them which passage you'll be reading for next time.

Whichever way you choose, here are things to cover in the first meeting:

1. Review the purpose for gathering (pp. 5-6).

2. Go over a few ground rules for discussion (p. 7).

3. Explain a few things about the Bible and Luke in particular (pp. 7-8).

4. Be sure everyone has a Bible.

STUDY 1. LUKE 1:1-38.
Preparing for Jesus.

Question 1

Luke was the only Gentile writer of the four Gospels. The Gospel of Luke is the first of a two-volume series that included the books of Acts. His writing shows him to be a highly educated man, one who wrote from a Greek background and point of view. Luke was probably a Gentile by birth, well educated in Greek culture, a physician by profession and a traveling companion of Paul's at various times. This book was probably written between A.D. 59 and 63.

In verses 1-4 he tells us that he wrote this Gospel to give the true and complete story of Jesus' life. He makes it clear that "he has done his homework" by investigating the story of Jesus with completeness, accuracy and thoroughness, and in an orderly fashion. Luke's purpose is set forth in verse 4, "so that Your Excellency may realize what assurance you have for the instruction you have received." The identity of Theophilus is not known for certain. He was probably a young Christian, or perhaps an interested seeker.

Question 2

In that day there was a great stigma attached to childlessness, especially since all health problems were decreed to be punishment for sins. So not only did people endure the suffering of their illness or barrenness but they had guilt attached to it as well.

Question 3

Zechariah had no doubt prayed for years that they would have a child. But it's unlikely that he would use this holy, awesome moment to make a personal request to God, especially as he was the emissary on behalf of his people. Furthermore, at his age it is unlikely that he would still be praying for a child. He must have prayed for the redemption of Israel—for the Messiah to come.

Question 4

John is to be great in the Lord's sight, as he is to live an ascetic life of discipline. The refusal to drink wine shows a special consecration and recalls the role of a prophet like Samuel (1 Sam 1:11). He will be empowered by the Spirit even from birth.

Question 5

Even with Gabriel's remarkable credentials Zechariah has a momentary lapse of faith. Gabriel is God's special archangel. He stands in God's presence and it is God who has sent him to bring the good news.

Question 6

The penalty (a supernatural act of being made mute) makes it impossible for Zechariah to complete his once in a lifetime priestly duty to the enormous multitude waiting for him to come out. Zechariah's momentary lapse is understandable, but he could not properly bless the people in view of this lapse. The penalty is not vindictive but allows the priest to reflect in silence on what God is doing in his life.

If you think your group would like to go a little deeper, you could follow this question up by asking, "When have you experienced a 'season of silence' in which you learned important things?"

Question 8

Mary was a virgin and betrothed to Joseph, from David's royal line. A betrothal was a legal relationship, thus more than an engagement. The two families would have a ceremony to celebrate this agreement to the marriage. For one more year she would live with her parents and they would be carefully chaperoned. After that he would take her to his home and have full responsibility for her. To break or violate a betrothal would require a divorce. The pregnancy would be scandalous. Mary no doubt was anxious over Joseph's reaction to her situation as well as that of their parents.

Question 9

Gabriel stresses Jesus' position (Son of God, Son of the Most High, ruler), his authority (seated on Israel's throne forever, ruler of a kingdom that will never end) and his divine ties (the Holy Spirit will come and over-shadow you). The Jews expected a messiah but not a "divine" one. It is clear even from Mary's reactions to Jesus in his early years, that she did not understand fully the angel's promise here to be a declaration of his deity. That understanding would come slowly, as it did for the disciples.

Question 10

The portrait Luke paints of Mary is significant. She takes God at his word, in contrast to Zechariah. She is favored by God, thoughtful, obedient, believing, worshipful and a faithful follower of God's law.

Question 11

Certainly hearing about Elizabeth's pregnancy would have lifted her faith as well as hearing the angel say, "Nothing is impossible with God" (v. 37).

Question 13

God chose the name John before the baby was conceived and told Zechariah to name him John in verse 13. In Zechariah's act of obedience God restored his speech.

Question 15

Luke wants us to understand that we cannot perceive Jesus correctly without understanding his divine origins. Christianity is based upon the supernatural because Christ came from heaven. However, Luke allows us to see that the human process of recognizing Jesus' true identity took time. Luke engages us in their slow process of discovery.

STUDY 2. LUKE 2.
Presenting Jesus.

Question 2

God chose to identify with his creation in the humblest of all possible ways. John the Baptist's birth was announced in the capital, at the temple, in the center of the Jewish nation. But Jesus arrives in rural obscurity. John is the child of a priest; Jesus belongs to Jews of average social status. The message is that God cares for all and identifies with all. Yet as humble as his birth is, it is accompanied by the attention of the heavenly host!

Question 5

The meaning of the word *Messiah* or *Christ* is "anointed one." In ancient Israel both persons and things consecrated to sacred purposes were anointed by having oil poured over them. The term *Messiah* or *Christ* referred to one anointed by God. The Jewish people believed Old Testament prophecy that pointed to a King and Savior (*Jesus* means "Savior") anointed by God to deliver them from their enemies. He was to come from the line of David (1 Chron 12:11-15). He was called "Son of Man" because he would be born a man (Dan 17:13-14). The Jewish people who did not recognize Jesus, however, had overlooked prophecy that their Messiah must suffer and die for the sins of the world (Is 53).

Question 7

We observe throughout the passage how careful the parents are to fulfill all the requirements of the law. They are faithful, observant Jews. Mary would later bring Jesus as a newborn to the temple because every male firstborn belonged to God and had to be offered to the Lord, so a substitute animal was offered. Because Mary and Joseph were poor, they offered two pigeons instead of a lamb. She also came to the temple after giving birth to Jesus to be made ceremonially clean. Furthermore, we see Mary and Joseph's response of faith in very difficult circumstances. They trusted God's word to be true even though they didn't understand it fully.

Question 8

To see Jesus is to see God's salvation offered to the whole world—Jews as well as Gentiles.

Question 10

Imagine what a contrast of emotions! One the one hand she would experience such joy in giving birth to this remarkable baby, on the other hand hearing that not only will her son be rejected, but a sword will one day pierce her heart as well. As confusing as this was to hear, how comforting it would be some thirty years later as she watched her son die on a cross, and then remembered what Simeon had told her. God was preparing Mary even then.

Questions 12-13

This experience happened in the springtime at Passover, which was an annual religious feast that took place in Jerusalem to celebrate Israel's deliverance from Egypt about 1300 B.C. It was a happy, festive time. On Joseph and Mary's return home they realized Jesus wasn't with their party. They returned to Jerusalem and found him listening to the teachers and then asking questions. The parents were astonished not only that their young son could hold his own with illustrious teachers of the law but that these teachers were fascinated by Jesus' depth of understanding. Nevertheless, Mary is hurt and distressed by the anxiety he has caused them. Jesus is equally astonished that his parents wouldn't know that he could be found in his father's house (the temple) teaching God's ways. It is significant that this clue to Jesus' identity and mission comes from Jesus himself. It is also significant that he reveals his unique relationship to God while in the temple. No religious Jew would *ever* call God their father! God was the father of Israel in a symbolic sense, but was considered too holy and unapproachable to call "my father." How fully Jesus understands his role at this point we are not told. What we do know is that even at twelve he had a remarkable sense of union with his father in heaven and of purpose.

STUDY 3. LUKE 3:21-23; 4:1-30.
The Power of Good over Evil.

Question 1

See also John 1:19-32. Was there a real dove that descended on Jesus during his baptism? Opinion is divided. The text says it was *like* a dove, which suggests that it was not a dove. However, Luke tells us that what descended was in bodily form so it had a visible entity. Whether the Spirit looked like a dove or descended in a manner from heaven like a dove is unclear. The important thing is that John knew this was the sign promised by God that the One he had been waiting for had arrived.

Question 2

It is hard to overemphasize the importance of this divine baptismal endorsement from heaven. God refers to Jesus as "my Son," "the one whom I love" and "with whom I am well pleased"; that, coupled with the Spirit's anointing, testifies that God both endorses Jesus and reveals the Spirit's enabling presence that comes in and through him from heaven. (The Spirit descended and *remained* on him.) This fresh awareness of his identity would strengthen him in the future as he would face constant opposition, hostility and rejection.

Question 3

Jesus does not accept baptism for the sake of his own sin. His participation in the rite reveals his willingness to take up humanity's cause in salvation (which will ultimately lead him to the cross). His identification with humanity is total. "He has borne our grief and carried our sorrows" as Isaiah says. He is also affirming John's ministry that repentance is necessary.

Questions 4-5

In this first temptation the devil is raising the question of whether God's word at Jesus' baptism and his provision can really be counted on. This is at an especially difficult time because Jesus is so hungry. But the temptation probably has more to do with trying to thwart Jesus' mission. Jesus didn't come to solve world hunger, as worthy as that goal is. Jesus' reply indicates that food can't fill our spiritual needs, but God can. He quoted Deuteronomy 8:3.

The Bible refers to Satan as an angelic being who led a heavenly revolt against God and consequently was cast out of heaven with his rebelling host of angels (2 Pet 2:4; Rev 12:7-8). Under his leadership, these angelic beings became known as demons, and are very organized in their schemes and attacks on human beings (Eph 6:12). Satan and his forces work to get us to worship him (Lk 4:7) and to prevent us from turning to God (Lk 4:8). Satan's defeat is promised in Genesis 3:15 and is completed at the cross of Christ (Col 2:15). He is still a force to be reckoned with until Christ returns to judge the earth (Mt 16:27). James 4:7 tells us to resist the devil (or demonic forces) as we seek God's will in our lives. This is what Jesus modeled in his own victory over Satan in Luke 4:1-13 (*Wycliffe Bible Commentary*).

Question 6

This was probably a vision. Satan offers Jesus an opportunity to grab power. But to do so would be to engage in false worship for it would put Jesus under Satan's domination. Though the devil has great power he does not have the authority to offer Jesus everything.

Question 7

Jesus as the Son of God is obedient to his father's will and refuses to be seduced into using his power or authority or "connections" for Satan's purposes.

Question 8

Jesus refused to dialogue with evil. He didn't explain, defend or process—rather he answered Satan's words with God's Word from Deuteronomy.

Question 9

Galilee, lying in the northern region of Israel, served as

the major ministry center for Jesus, with the city of Capernaum being his headquarters. Because of Jesus' teaching his fame began spreading throughout the region. When he returned to his hometown of Nazareth, the people would have heard the reports of his ministry and the excitement he generated everywhere he went. Their initial reaction must have been one of pride and curiosity.

Question 11

It is significant that Jesus read from a messianic passage of Scripture from Isaiah. The text speaks about the coming Messiah and his mission. Jesus declares that the day all Jews have waited for, the coming of Messiah and the ushering in of God's kingdom, has finally come. After almost two thousand years of promise, stretching all the way back to Abraham, Jesus claims that the promises of a prophet like Isaiah are now being realized in him! He was the "anointed one" because the Spirit of God was upon him. He would preach good news to the poor (not just the poverty-stricken but the spiritually needy). He would release captives (by forgiving their sins) and he would restore sight to the blind (both physically and spiritually).

Question 12

Knowing their thoughts, Jesus answers in three ways. First, he cites a proverb that indicates they want him to prove his credentials by performing a miracle. But miracles, in the end, never convince someone who does not want to come to God. Second, Jesus quotes the proverb that a prophet is not honored in his home. Third, Jesus recalls the history of Israel in the time of Elijah and Elisha (1 Kings 17—18; 2 Kings 5:1-14). This was a period in which unbelief, idolatry and unfaithfulness were rampant. So God offered mercy to those outside the Jewish circle in the Gentile regions. The price of rejecting God's message is severe: he will simply offer grace to other locales. The townspeople are furious at the suggestion that Gentiles might be blessed while Israel receives nothing. Jesus' point is that blessing refused is tragic.

STUDY 4. LUKE 4:31–5:11.
The Power of Jesus Released.

Question 1
Jewish teachers did not dare present their own interpretations of the passage, but quoted former interpreters. But Jesus gave authoritative interpretations without quoting anyone.

Question 3
There was an unusual amount of demonic activity in Jesus' day as Satan was mounting his attack against Jesus. Episodes like this one reveal the deep cosmic struggle between the forces of evil and Jesus. This is Jesus' second encounter with evil since the temptation. The man in this passage is threatened directly by this demonic possessive force. The "us" that the demon refers to could mean "have you come to destroy all demons?" (1 Jn 3:8) or perhaps he thinks that his influ-

ence is so strong over the man that Jesus couldn't exorcise the demon without destroying the man he possesses. The fact that we are told the man remained uninjured seems to suggest the latter meaning.

Question 4

By accurately naming Jesus as "the Holy One of God" the demon draws attention that this is a battle of cosmic proportions and the demon makes it clear that Jesus is on God's side and the demons are not. What a picture of Jesus' power that he is able to remove the evil presence while preserving the man (though the demon tries to hurt him by throwing him on the ground). But that is why Jesus came—to "set the captives free." The demonic realm is fully aware of who Jesus is (they recognize his authority over them; they believe he is the Son of God and Messiah), yet they choose to rebel instead of worship and obey God.

Jesus might have silenced the demon for several reasons: he didn't want the revelation of his divinity to be proclaimed by evil sources but rather by himself; he didn't want his supernatural powers to be attributed to demons rather than God.

Question 5

Jesus' overwhelming authority is revealed. Jesus' power over evil is not limited to spiritual forces. His healing of Peter's mother-in-law shows his authority over disease and thus his authority over life! The way Jesus rebuked her serious illness doesn't suggest she is demonically possessed but rather that all that destroys and wounds us is ultimately the fruit of the enemy's plan and desire.

Question 8

Jesus' ministry was driven not by need alone but by strategy, goals and following God's will. It must have been difficult to leave but he had a sense of urgency about the mission God had given to him.

Question 9

Lake Gennesaret is the name the Jews often gave to the Sea of Galilee. A freshwater lake, 13x8 miles, 680 feet below sea level, it had nine large townships on its shores and the fish were exported all over the empire.

The disciples were no doubt busy cleaning the nets rather than listening to Jesus.

Question 11

They had been up all night and were no doubt exhausted and discouraged by the lack of fish. Net cleaning was a laborious process that involved removing by hand all the debris. Peter would think it was an impossible request since now the fish were at a deeper level by daybreak. To tell experienced fishermen that they must get their clean nets dirty all over again would have been very frustrating. And what did an ex-carpenter know about fishing anyway?

Question 13

Peter knew he had witnessed an incredible miracle. His sense of sin suggests that Peter had a bad attitude toward both Jesus' requests. Because this miracle was in Peter's area of expertise he realizes Jesus is Lord of even his professional life.

Questions 14-15

Up until now Peter, James and John had been disciples of Jesus while continuing their fishing business. Now Jesus is asking them to leave their fishing careers and become his disciples. This was a difficult request and a great step of faith on their part. But the fact that Jesus has demonstrated his authority in such powerful ways convinced them that obedience to Jesus' authority was the only appropriate response. Furthermore, their great catch of fish that day would have supported their families for a long time.

STUDY 5. LUKE 5:12-31.
The Power of Jesus Revealed.

Question 3

It is extremely significant that Jesus touched this leper, for Jews believed to do so made them ceremonially unclean. Furthermore, no one touched a leper for fear of contracting the dreaded disease. But Mark 1:41 tells us that Jesus had "compassion" on this man's plight. He didn't have to touch him to heal him, but Jesus knew this man had not been touched by a well person since he contracted the disease. He needed healing emotionally as well as physically. Jesus probably also wanted to demonstrate to him and to anyone watching that he was truly healed!

Question 4

First, if the cured leper simply presented himself to the people they would run for the hills. They wouldn't wait to see if his symptoms were really gone. By going to the priest and making the required offering he could be reinstated in society. Second, Jesus knew that if the man told everyone about his healing (which Mark 1:45 tells us he did!) that it would make it more difficult for Jesus to minister openly in crowded areas.

Question 6

The Pharisees were a dominant religious group in Jesus day who believed the Messiah was coming. They were conservative theologically, but not politically. They would approve of an uprising to free themselves from Roman rule. They were a legalistic and separatist group who strictly, but sometimes hypocritically, kept the law of Moses and the "tradition of the elders" (rabbinic commentary on the law). The Pharisees numbered about 6,000 in Palestine and were respected by the people as the "unofficial religious leaders." Their interpretation of the laws, handed down as traditions for generations, was regarded by them to be as authoritative as the Scripture itself. Some of them were pretentious and some were godly.

The teachers of the law were scribes, or lawyers. They interpreted the Scriptures and how to apply the law to everyday life.

The Sadducees were a Jewish party that represented the wealthy and sophisticated classes. They were largely in Jerusalem and made the temple and its administration their primary interest. Being more worldly and politically minded they didn't accept the Pharisees' belief in the supernatural such as the resurrection.

They had power in the Jewish governing body called the Sanhedrin, but their views set them against the Pharisees.

The key is that all of these dignitaries had come from every village of Galilee and Judea, and some even from Jerusalem! This must have been a planned event and there were a good number. This is no casual get-together. It is a formal investigation to see who this Jesus really is. This must have been a large house to be able to accommodate so many people.

Question 8

In Jesus' day people thought all illness and physical handicaps were due to God's displeasure because a sin had been committed.

Question 9

Only God could forgive sins. Of course that is the very point Jesus is indirectly making.

Question 10

Jesus says that to show them he had the authority to forgive sins he would heal the man. Blasphemy, the claim to be God, was considered by the Pharisees to be the worst sin a person could commit because it offended God's authority and majesty. Jewish theology did not even allow for the Messiah to claim God's authority to forgive sin.

Question 11

Even Jesus' critics must have been praising God. Verse 26 says, "Everyone was amazed."

Question 12

One of Luke's great themes throughout his Gospel is that salvation is offered to all men and women. There is no one beyond the reach of Jesus' ability to heal and save.

Question 13

Some believe that Levi was most likely baptized by John (Lk 3:12-13), made a commitment to God and started cleaning up his accounts. He no doubt longed for the kingdom but thought he could never qualify because of his past life of extorting money.

STUDY 6. LUKE 6:27-45.
The Plan for True Living.

Discussion Starter

The truth is, no one can live the Christian life freely without God's Spirit helping us.

Question 1

We are to love our enemies because it is the essence of God's character. We are to practice love and not revenge. Christian love is not basically an emotion but an act of the will. It is to seek the highest good of our enemies! In these verses Jesus is taking a new approach to the Old Testament law: "The Law of Moses laid down the right and duties of justice—what each person owed another. For example, the Law required penalties proportionate to the crime and fair repayment of loans. Jesus does not reject the Mosaic definition of justice; fair is still fair in law court and marketplace. But in private relations between individuals, Jesus lays down a new law" (Diana Shick, *Grace Under Pressure: Studies from the Book of Luke* [Reston, Va.: Creative Living International, 1990], p. 95).

Question 5

In light of the forthcoming hostility and persecution that his disciples were to face this would be a timely message for them.

Questions 6-8

In other passages Jesus tells us that we are to be discerning—which is a form of judgment. What we are to avoid is passing judgment on someone by declaring what he deserves; we are not to desire revenge. Jesus warns us against the kind of judgment that declares a person deserves to be hated and punished for hating or mistreating or robbing us (6:27-29). That kind of judgment and condemnation is the opposite of love and mercy and forgiveness. Rather a nonjudgmental, accepting, forgiving, generous person is likely to be treated in the same way.

Question 9

Their very diverse backgrounds, the friction of traveling together and their seemingly competitive natures could easily lead to conflict. Although all of them were Galileans except for Judas the traitor (who was a Judean), they were very different men. Peter seems to have been a bit impulsive, Jesus called John and his brother James "Sons of thunder" which suggests they had quick tempers and strong personalities. Matthew, whose other name was Levi, had been an ex-customs officer and a despised outcast who extorted money from his own people. Thomas tended to be pessimistic and doubting. Simon the Zealot had belonged to a radical political group of revolutionaries who worked for the overthrow of Roman control of the Jewish people. Imagine how he would feel about Matthew before becoming a follower of Christ! But Jesus doesn't want cookie-cutter Christians! He wants us to reproduce his godly character in our own very diverse personalities without squelching us.

Question 10

Their love for each other would secure the continuation of the church and would convince seekers they were genuine followers of Jesus and that he was truly God.

Question 11

Jesus seems to be suggesting that unless we deal first with ourselves then we won't be able to perceive others aright. Once we've dealt with out own problems and faults, then our own motives and perceptions will be clearer.

Question 13

"Judge not" is not an absolute prohibition about making any judgments, otherwise we would lack discernment in how to minister to others. Rather our discernment should make us prayerful and compassionate toward the other person.

STUDY 7. LUKE 8:22-56.
The Power to Overcome Suffering.

Question 1

The fishing boat had several oars on each side and it also had sails. It was big enough to hold at least thirteen men plus their equipment and a great deal of fish. The text says they "sailed away" implying that the weather was good and there was no hint of an impending storm.

They awakened Jesus because they feared for their own lives and for his. They were in real danger of drowning if the boat was swamped, but they certainly never imagined what he would do! The contrast could not be greater as to the humanity and divinity of Jesus in this story. There he was in the boat, asleep no doubt due to exhaustion from constant ministry, utterly human and tired and in the next moment commanding a storm to be still.

Question 2

The fact that Jesus rebuked the wind suggests that Satan may have been behind this storm. But what Jesus wanted them to understand is that his word could absolutely be trusted.

Question 3

Remember that these men were fanatic monotheists. Yet ordering creation to obey was something only God could do. How could the tired, sleepy Jesus have done this? They believed Jesus was Messiah but they were wrestling with whether he could also be God. They were familiar with the psalms and Psalm 89:8-9. Psalm

65:5-8 must have also come to mind. Jesus is enlarging their faith as well as their conception of him.

Question 5

It's almost impossible to distinguish the man from the demons since he is totally under demonic control. Yet Jesus appeals to the man's own sense of identity. He gives dignity and honor to the man God created.

Question 7

In spite of the fact that they saw the former demoniac clothed, in his right mind and sitting at the feet of Jesus, instead of being amazed and thrilled, they were angry about their economic loss (the pigs). If Jesus cared so much about one man, surely he would have cared about them too. But they never gave Jesus the chance.

Question 8

Clearly this man was waiting for Jesus when he got off the boat because he was absolutely desperate. The synagogue elders and some Jewish religious leaders hated Jesus by this point and some had already determined to kill him. Turning to Jesus for help and believing in him could have resulted in Jairus being ousted from his duties at the synagogue.

Question 11

She was terrified to be discovered because she was considered unclean and her touch would have made Jesus ceremonially unclean. The crowd would have been enraged that she stood in their midst. She no doubt expected to be dealt with harshly.

Question 12

He calls her "daughter" which probably meant she was a younger woman. He publicly commends her faith and pronounces her well.

Question 15

Perhaps the reason Jesus told the parents not to tell what had happened to their daughter is that he wanted them to focus on her needs and provide her protection from the crowd. Also the publicity of Jesus' miracles made it increasingly hard to minister to large crowds.

STUDY 8. LUKE 9:10-36.
Who Do You Say That I Am?

Question 1

Bethsaida was the fishing village where the first four fisherman came from, as did Philip and Nathanael. For six of them it was going home. The disciples were no doubt longing for rest and time alone with Jesus, but Jesus had compassion on the crowd.

Question 5

Jesus wants them to learn to shepherd their flock by caring for their needs. However, the main point they must learn is that all of their power for ministry comes through Jesus and his father. No matter how inadequate they might feel, if they gave it all to Jesus he could make it enough to feed 5,000!

Question 7

Peter is now realizing that Jesus is more than a unique prophetic teacher who reveals God's ways. Jesus is the deliverer, a special agent of God, who is ushering in a new era. The disciples had no trouble believing Jesus was the promised Messiah. But it would take time for these fierce monotheists to see that the Messiah was a divine-human figure as well. Peter is on the way toward understanding the deity of Christ, but it's probably not until the resurrection appearances and the ascension of Jesus that the disciples grasp Christ's full identity.

Question 8

To have even a blossoming understanding of Christ's deity was considered blasphemy and punishable by death. Jesus needed the disciples to understand his mission and especially the cross that awaited him. He wanted to communicate certain facts about his mission before it got bandied about in public. Furthermore, John 6:15 tells us that after the feeding of the 5,000 many wanted to make him king.

Question 9

The disciples must have thought that victory and power were right around the corner. Jesus will be king and they will rule with him! They would be baffled by Jesus' insistence that he must die.

Question 10

Disciples are like their teachers. Whether the path leads to losing one's life for the sake of Jesus (which all the disciples would experience except John), being rejected or not being ashamed to be identified with Christ, true followers need to understand that the Christian life will not be stress-free. It will involve self-denial and freely serving others, in essence following Christ's example.

Question 14

The difficulty is that Peter still hasn't fully grasped the absolute uniqueness of Jesus. He seems to see Jesus as another great figure like Moses and Elijah. His suggestion understates Jesus' relationship to his two witnesses.

Question 15

The voice from heaven is God's and it is definitive. They need to listen to Jesus so they can understand his uniqueness, call and destiny to suffer. They need to *listen to Jesus,* let Jesus explain to them who he really is ("my son") and serve him.

Other Books by Rebecca Manley Pippert

Hope Has Its Reasons

This is a book geared for people who want honest answers to honest questions. Rebecca Pippert examines the persistently human longings that all of us share about significance, meaning, life and truth, and the search for security. Only after she unravels the core of the real problem that plagues us does she explore how Christ can meet our longings and solve our human crisis. There are no canned formulas or saccharine clichés. Realism rings in the stories she tells and the ideas she pursues. In doing so she leads us beyond the search for our own significance to the reasons for our hope in discovering God.

A Heart for God

How can God use the difficulties and sufferings in our lives to build character and deepen our faith? The biblical David faced some desperate circumstances and some tough choices. So do we, day by day. The author shows us how God is able to use the everyday grit and glory of our lives to shape a holy life within us. Using David as her guide she helps us understand the way Christian virtue is developed in our souls and vices are rooted out. We learn how we, like David, can choose the good, overcome temptation and grow to be one who has a heart for God.

Transformation

Would you like to move from despair to hope? Would you like to transform your feelings of fear to faith? Would you like to turn envy into compassion? The Bible shows how David turned these negative emotions in his life into godly character qualities. In this Christian Basics Bible Study, based on the Bible's account of David and the book *A Heart for God*, you'll investigate David's life, choices, mistakes and triumphs. Then you'll discover how you can make the same transformation in your own life.